Sophia May Eckley

Easter roses

Sophia May Eckley

Easter roses

ISBN/EAN: 9783741195044

Manufactured in Europe, USA, Canada, Australia, Japa

Cover: Foto ©Andreas Hilbeck / pixelio.de

Manufactured and distributed by brebook publishing software (www.brebook.com)

Sophia May Eckley

Easter roses

EASTER ROSES.

EASTER ROSES.

BY

SOPHIA MAY ECKLEY,

Authoress of the " Oldest of the Old World," " Light on Dark Days." &c.

" And the desert shall rejoice and blossom as the rose."
ISAIAH XXXV. 1.

LONDON:
SIMPKIN, MARSHALL, AND CO., STATIONERS' HALL COURT.
BATH: R. E. PEACH, BRIDGE STREET.

MDCCCLXIV.

Inscribed to

A. B. L. G.

"Where fall the tears of Love, the rose appears."

CONTENTS.

The Rose of Sharon ... ...
Sea-Treasures ... ...
" Why ? " ... ...
Mizpah ... ...
Snow-Treasures ... ...
The Passing Bell ... ...
" If need be " ... ...
Awake ! ... ...

Collect for Easter Day.

Almighty God, who through Thine only begotten Son Jesus Christ, hast overcome Death, and opened unto us the gate of everlasting life; we humbly beseech Thee, that, as by Thy special grace preventing us, Thou dost put into our minds good desires, so by Thy continual help, we may bring the same to good effect; through Jesus Christ our Lord, who liveth and reigneth with Thee and the Holy Ghost, ever one God, world without end. Amen.

PRAYER OF MARY QUEEN OF SCOTS.

Domine Deus, speravi in te,
O care mi Jesu nunc libera me;
In dura Catena,
In misera pœna,
Desidero te;
Languendo,
Gemendo,
Genuflectendo,
Adoro,
Imploro,
Ut liberes me!

TRANSLATION.

O Lord my God, I hope in Thee,
O Jesu mine, deliver me;
In heavy chains, in dreary pains,
Longing, I desire Thee—
Fainting ever, groaning ever,
Still to Thee, I bend the knee;
Thus adoring, thus imploring.
That Thou would'st deliver me.

S. M. E.

"The Rose of Sharon."

"The flowers appear on the earth; the time of the singing of birds is come, and the voice of the turtle is heard in our land."

SONG OF SOLOMON ii. 12.

A brilliant Rose, and Lily pure and white,
Let us this Easter morn in one unite,
Binding them fast with cords of mighty love,
That sever not, but reach to Heaven above.
A symbol this ! Christ is the Sharon rose,
That blossoms still, tho' storms and night may close
Around the dreary wastes of life—still he
Will find that rose, who seeks it faithfully.
The Lily typifies Christ's Church so fair,
That ever simple purity should wear,
And like the Lily breathe a sweetness round,
That may not in another flower be found.
Christ and His Church—Aye, let us bind them fast,
Until they meet before God's Throne at last.

ALICE.

"The Rose of Sharon."

"I am the Rose of Sharon, and the Lily of the Valleys."

AS the traveller wanders over the dreary wastes of Palestine, he does not look in vain for the "rose of Sharon." The scarlet anemone blossoms even now in wild luxuriance over the otherwise stony, barren soil; and this is the flower which is held traditionally to be the "Rose of Sharon."

Even the Bedouin Arab holds it in reverence. They are called by them "the Saviour's blood-drops," a name which the early Christians gave them.

Long tracts of wastes are relieved of their dreary monotony by these brilliant flowers.

The "Rose of Sharon" then, may not be an inappropriate emblem for an Easter offering. Isaiah sang of the desolation of Zion, and of the final flourishing of Christ's kingdom, under the beautiful simile of the *Rose*—"The desert shall rejoice and blossom as the Rose."

And Solomon employs the same figure to illustrate the mutual love of Christ and His Church—"I am the rose of Sharon and the lily of the valleys."

We have lately been commemorating the solemn interval of our Saviour's

Cross and Passion; that sad season past, let us now bring the "Rose of Sharon" and the "lily of the valleys," and bind them in closer union—Christ and His Church.

Christ, the "Rose of Sharon," blossoming in triumphant splendour over this world's dreary wastes.

No valley so lonely, no bye-path so devious, but this rose may be discovered if we seek for it, even among the brambles and thickets of life's dreariest pathways.

And the lilies of the valley—these symbolize Christ's true followers growing beside Him, in simplicity, purity, and meekness. Like the lilies, clinging lightly to earth and its transient, fading pleasures. Like the lilies, which exhale their sweetness, distinctly perceptible from the other woodland flowers; thus should the Christian in life and conversation breathe the graces of a renewed nature, which should be distinctly perceptible, and perfume the atmosphere in which he moves—" In the world, yet not of the world."

Like the lilies too in innocency of life—gentle, lovely, kind; that they may not only profess, but "adorn the doctrine of God our Saviour, in all things."

Sea-Treasures.

Awake and sing, ye that dwell in dust."

"But now is Christ risen from the dead, and become the first fruits of them that slept."
1 Cor. xv. 20.

"Ye faithful souls who Jesus know,
  If risen indeed with Him ye are,
Superior to the joys below,
  This resurrection power declare,
Your faithful, holy tempers prove,
  By actions show your sins forgiven,
And seek the glorious things above,
  And follow Christ your Head to Heaven."

Chant on ye voices of the sea,
  Sweep the dark wave-chords light,
As in your floating minstrelsy,
  Ye sing the Hymn of Night.

Sea-Treasures.

"The earth is full of thy riches, so is the great and wide sea."

OW strikingly King David appeals to the imagination in the Psalms! His spirit was always rejoicing in the beauties of the natural world, nor was he ever weary of singing of the goodness and power of God in His beautiful creations.

The moon, the stars, the earth, the flowers, the sea, were all inexhaustible themes to him. And the Poets, the Evangelists, the Prophets of the Bible, drew all their analogies from the book of Nature. So did the Saviour and His Apostles, yet how little do Christians now make the God of nature, the interpreter of the God of Revelation.

There is so much materialism in the Christianity of the present day—so little spirituality.

Yet let us listen to another eloquent voice of Nature, the "great and wide sea." In the ocean, we read the Memoirs of the soul! The murmur of the waves' deep octave, its increasing roll and swell, the music of its ripples—all find a simile in these restless, surging unsatisfied souls of ours.

The sun's golden chariot dashing through the breakers, trails daylight in the frothy wake, and it is sunrise!

Then follows the dazzling splendour

of the jewelled noon-day, when sky and sea like emerald and turquoise, seem to reflect the pavements of the golden city. Then dark ocean night, when only the phosphorescent jewel gilds the wave-crest; or the moon and her starry train drop their golden links down into the fathomless depths.

Sunrise typifies the morning of life—truth, hope, joy. Noon-day, when prosperity and happiness seem to be in our grasp—when we believe in the shadows we chase, and take them for the substantial and enduring—when we clothe ourselves in the gauzy garments of illusion, and refuse to be unclothed, —when Heaven seems to have stooped to earth, and mingles her strain with the changeful waves and currents of life, even as the turquoise and emerald mingle their colours in the noon-day of the sea.

Then comes the night of the soul, when only the jewels of Faith and God's Love, gem the crests of sorrow's mightiest billows.

Even so the soul has her morning hours, her noonday hours, her twilight, and her midnight hours.

The sea too has her own scenery. Her lights and shadows, her ever changeful moods. Never one moment the same—an endless gallery of moving pictures.

Every freak of sunlight revealing some new-born beauty. Even her mists building bridges, phantom-ships, and illusive landscapes, which fade and dissolve as soon as we approach them.

Has not the soul just such scenery-chambers, phantom hopes, visionary landscapes, picture galleries, *mirages*, life illusions, empty dreams, for ever unfulfilled?

The sea has her dangerous shoals and reefs too, more dreaded by the mariner than the tempest's fury.

Has not the soul also her dangerous reefs, and sunken rocks of temptations, her gilded snares, her syren voices?

Lastly, she has her beacon light, shining on that distant calm shore, where the murmur of celestial waves lulls the weary soul to her final rest and peace.

In the sunrise at sea, we behold too another beautiful figure of our Risen Lord!

Is He not the " Sun of righteousness," even here rising " with healing in His wings," over the wastes of spiritual apathy and death, illuming the soul in her dark hours, and gilding each wave-crest of earthly event and transitory joy, with jewels whose lustre is never dimmed? Keep these jewels untarnished here on earth, fellow Pilgrim, so will they be meet to be set in the diadem of thy everlasting life, —and take heed too that no man take thy crown.

"Because thou hast kept the word of my patience, I also will keep thee from the hour of temptation, which shall come upon all the world, to *try* them that dwell upon the earth." *Rev.* iii. 10.

For "blessed is the man that *endureth* temptation, for when he is tried, he shall receive the crown of life, which the Lord hath promised to them that love Him." *James* i. 12.

" For He maketh the storm to cease, so that the waves thereof are still." *Psalm* cvii. 29.

"Why?"

"Nay but, O man, who art thou that repliest against God?"

ROM. ix. 20.

"For as in Adam all die, even so in Christ shall all be made alive."

1 COR. xv. 22.

" When sorrowing, o'er some stone I bend,
Which covers all that was a friend,
And from his hand, his voice, his smile,
Divides me for a little while,
My Saviour marks the tears I shed,
For " Jesus wept " o'er Lazarus dead.

And oh ! when I have safely past
Through every conflict but the last,
Still, Lord, unchanging watch beside
My dying bed, for Thou hast died;
Then point to realms of cloudless day,
And wipe the latest tear away."

"Why?"

"Verily thou art a God that hidest thyself, O God of Israel, the Saviour."

WHY reason ye these things in your hearts? asked the Saviour. Can ye not become as little children in your faith?

The reasoning of man in religion is often his own self-glorification.

When we can discern through reason or human speculation, *why* God saw fit to send His only begotten Son into this world, to redeem it upon the Cross—when we can answer *why* one planet has eight moons, another four, and our own but one—when, through reason, we can learn *why* God permits evil to triumph over good, the wicked to prosper, the virtuous and innocent to suffer—then may we dare to question His mysterious Providences towards us. Not until then.

"Nay but, O man, who art thou that repliest against God?" asks St. Paul; and yet, ever since Time began, the world's universal question, and the heart's lone wail, has been, "Why?"

Why hast Thou thus dealt with me? asks the invalid. Why has the flower of my life been taken from me? asks the mourning mother, as the grave closes over her loveliest child. Alas!

she stamps upon the earth-mould, and crushes the flower of resignation with her withering question, "Why?"

The Good Shepherd has taken her little lamb in his arms, that the mother may follow. Over the rough passes of the Eastern mountains, the shepherd may be seen to-day, carrying the lamb of his flock, and often he places one in the fold to allure the stray mother, who has wandered away over the steep ravine, attracted by some greener pasturage.

Can we not apply this lovely simile to the death of little children? Saint Gregory thus alludes to this beautiful emblem—"The Good Shepherd will at one time give his sheep rest, and at another, direct them. With his staff, seldom, but more generally with his pipe; but the lambs he carries in his bosom." The father loses his son, shot down in defence of his country's flag. The most promising of the band is taken; the other, whose life is one perpetual sorrow and disappointment, is left—why?

"Verily thou art a God that hidest thyself, O God of Israel, the Saviour."

It is well for us the answer is hidden. "Oh, ye of little faith, wherefore dost thou doubt?" asks our risen Lord this Easter season.

"Behold I shew you a mystery," wrote St. Paul. The resurrection of the body was as impenetrable a mystery to him as to us, and yet he believed it, taught it, and asked not *why*.

We must be content now to "see through a glass darkly." If we are *children* lowly and meek, then we are *heirs*. This only is the condition of our heir-ship—" Except ye become as little children, ye cannot inherit the kingdom of heaven."

The cold elective light of reason may glitter, may delude, but it cannot illuminate, or even cast one ray of light, to disclose one *reason* for what God has chosen to hide beneath the curtain of His mysterious providences.

Not that we should not "give a reason of the faith that is in us," with meekness and fear, but we should avoid that perpetual rock of stumbling—the heart's question—" *Why?* "

The sun we cannot gaze upon with the naked eye, and even when eclipsed, it must be veiled to us by a smoked or colored glass, to enable us to gaze upon it. Through the darkened glass only can the eye look upon its shrouded splendour.

Thus in our earthly experience, let the Christian be content to behold his Father hidden, and to see his Saviour through the glass darkly, waiting patiently for that Easter morning of which this season is only typical.

Then shall we see Him as He is. Then shall we be able to bear the unveiled glory of Him, who through life's darkest glooms, most perplexing conflicts, and bitterest sorrows, has walked beside us, "touched with the feeling of our infirmities," bearing our sins, and carrying our sorrows.

Though here we say meekly, with eyes streaming to heaven, yet in faith, —"Verily thou art a God that *hidest*

thyself, O God of Israel, the Saviour."
But ask no more the vain question—
"*Why?*"

"Mizpah."

"For though I be absent in the flesh, yet am I with you in the spirit."—Col. ii. 5.

"Set your affection on things above, not on things on the earth."—Col. iii. 2.

"Yet though thou wear'st the glory of the sky,
Wilt thou not keep the same beloved *name*,—
The same fair thoughtful brow, and gentle eye,
Lovelier in heaven's sweet climate, yet the same?"

"Yet what binds us friend to friend,
But that soul with soul can blend?
Soul-like were those hours of yore,
Let us walk in soul once more."

"Mizpah."

"The Lord watch between me and thee, when we are absent one from the other."

CHRIST is no longer absent from His church—He is risen to day. Let us retrace our thoughts to Jerusalem—to the lonely disciples, who on their journey to Emmaus, were talking over the sad events of the past week. We may fancy ourselves one of that sorrowing group, a listener to their sad discourse.

Regrets, no doubt, mingled with their words. They wished now they had listened more attentively to that voice that "spake as never man spake." They wished they had not questioned His divine mysteries—had loved Him more faithfully, and served Him better.

Now He had left them, and the weary blank of absence had succeeded to the thrilling events of His last hours on earth.

But we are told that Christ appeared to them on their way, walked with them, and joined in their conversation, veiling Himself to their material senses. "Their eyes were holden that they should not know him."

He saw "they were sad," yet He did not reveal Himself until He had thoroughly tried their faith.

He discerned the "questions" agitating their hearts too, and said unto them—"Why do thoughts arise in your hearts?" Why do ye doubt my presence?

The Saviour doubtless concealed His identity at first, to prove how far His disciples were capable of recognising His *spiritual* presence, and to what extent they depended upon the material impressions of sense to aid them in their recognition of Him.

"Behold, I am with you always, even unto the end of the world." This was the consoling doctrine He had taught when He was preparing them for His departure. "Absent in body, and present in spirit," says St. Paul, animated by the same cheering faith.

"For though I be absent in the

flesh, yet am I with you in the spirit," he says again, recognising throughout his ministry, the blessed doctrine of the unbroken spiritual intimacy of those who love, and are separated *bodily*.

It is the spiritual eye only that can perceive this truth.

The spiritual life of the affections is happily independent of the bodily presence.

Whether we apply these comforting assurances in the last farewells of death, or to the greetings and partings of the present life, we are emboldened to believe, and to cling more tenaciously than ever to the spiritual and growing life of the affections "when we are absent one from the other."

Mingled ever in the burden of the

"*Mizpah.*" 41

Psalm of Life is the mournful cadence "Farewell."

It weaves its plaintive minor into every song of life—to meet, to love, to part, is the common experience of every day.

But there are loves celestial and loves terrestrial—"the glory of the celestial is one, and the glory of the terrestrial is another." Some partings are a temporary Death! Only the celestial love—that which is born of God—survives all loss, defies all absence. *That* only holds its faith and allegiance through absence, and through Death. Such only can have a foretaste of the Spiritual life of Love beyond the grave.

Love, where it is true, must bear the

impress of the "celestial"—then it can never die.

But the most precious gem, is the one most frequently counterfeited, and strange as it may appear, there are persons who prefer the radiant glitter of a false jewel, to the barbaric splendour of a genuine unpolished gem! There are those who prefer in Art a fresh copy of some old master, to the old and faded original. Such persons live and die with Love a stranger to their souls.

But Christ is risen, Rise with Him! His walk with His Disciples to Emmaus witnesses to us the hopeful faith of His continual presence.

"Behold I am with you always, even unto the end of the world."—"I am the Resurrection and the Life." He is with His children now, and from Him we learn that neither absence nor death can separate us from Him, or from the loving and the loved on earth's changeful shore.

Snow-Treasures.

"Hast thou entered into the treasures of the snow?"
Job xxxviii. 22.

UNDER the snow, the crocus blooms,
'Neath the glacier cliff low lies
The oft exiled Soldanella,
Born from the tears of ice.

The sun that melts the cold ice-cliff,
To refresh that alpine flower,
Is the same smile of God, that warms
The heart in her dreary hour.

This is the lesson of life to learn,
The gardens of earth to prove,
E'en flowers our humble teachers are,
In lessons of God's sweet love.

S. M. E.

Snow-Treasures.

"He scattereth the hoar-frost like ashes. He casteth forth his ice like morsels; who can stand before his cold?"

IS ice like morsels! Switzerland is a great metaphorical church! She has aisles of glittering frost; galleries of glacial architecture, draped with silvery snow, and fringed with the prismatic icicle. She has altars of amethystine rock. She has her ceaseless anthem from a thousand rills; all in perfect harmony, not a discord marks her unity.

She only pleads one more acknowledgement, and that — the soul's "Amen."

Between the lofty peaks of the Wetter-horn, and the Engel-horn — awful peaks! — amid the sublime solitudes of the Swiss Oberland, the most beautiful glacier in all Switzerland cuts its way. Like a superb chrystallized river, it rises in regions of eternal snow, and is fed by countless streams, which freeze into ice-pyramids of incredible height.

The under current, swelling to rich streams, bears fertilizing strength to the green valleys below. Thus the utility of this phenomenon enhances our appreciation of its wondrous beauty.

Down the sides of the ravine through which the glacier passes, the verdure is dwarfed, though green, and often the Anemone, the Rhododendron, and the pale mystic star of the Soldanella luxuriate among cool shadows.

The daphne, too, is found here with her coronet of pink blossoms, and the *gentiana-glacialis*, with erect stern blue crown, clustering here and there in isolated seclusion.

Flowers in the wilderness of everlasting snows—love in death!

But this is not all the picture. The wrinkled sides of the hoary cliffs above, are embroidered with silver meshes of gushing rills; while further down, the armies of the dark fir forests open their ranks to make way for this mighty river to pass.

Amid this solemn scenery, I paused before a cave of magic beauty. It was chiselled by the hand of sunshine in an ice-wave above me.

Down a cavern of twenty feet in depth, I gazed. The vault of metallic blue dripped with icicles of prismatic beauty. Below, a melting, ever moving stream flowed on in her loving errand to the world.

A lesson of Life, Death and Immortality, I found typified in this frozen picture.

There was no life except the brief day of the flowers—no human habitation—no children's voices, nor lowing cattle; not even the flutter of an insect's wing. The wind seemed to moan a funeral dirge, as she bore her cold kiss from unexplored realms of the ice-world above.

As the glacier cuts its path through the gorge, tall pines, stately oaks, and tender saplings are often mowed down, though the little flower is passed by unscathed. On the margin of one of these glacier waves, a pale soldanella grew. This virgin beauty of the Alps! Her delicate head well poised on the wiry stem that firmly clung to the crumbling soil. God tempers the wind to each shorn lamb of the flock, I thought, and supplies even this little flower with strength to resist the Alpine storms. Hope blooming on the soil of death and desolation!

A lesson of faith, too, I found here. The wind swayed the gentle form of my flower, as she clustered under a huge pyramid of ice. Even from the icicle above, were distilled refreshing drops to feed her thirsty petals. Thus the winds of adversity pass by unscathed the faithful and patient sufferer; and even from the death-wave of bereavement, often distils in gentle dew, God's refreshing grace.

Above me the lofty pinnacles of the "Angel Peaks" rose as if in flight, to bear some message from earth's lone valleys to heaven. Thus faith soars upward from the ice-fields of death and desolation to the gardens of the Lord.

Nature's plaintive voices are always pleading for us, and crying, "Awake and sing, ye that dwell in dust!" Have we not a lesson of humility here to learn? Do we not more than in one sense "dwell in dust?" Are we not now in our prison of dust? Are not these souls of ours wrapt in garments of perishable dust, and do we not "cleave unto them?" Do we not die and return to dust? "Awake then and sing, ye that dwell in dust!" Sing of God's love, and sing our risen Lord; and let these Alpine voices whisper to us—life *in* death—life *from* death, and life *through* death!

Close to the ice-cliff grows the flower. From out the sorrow springs the "heart's-ease" of resignation. From the frozen drift flows the refreshing stream. From the ice of affliction, the dew of God's mercy.

And death? It is but a *name*. There is no death in nature. It is only life putting on new forms, new garments. The germ is *buried* in the flower. The water is imprisoned in the ice. The spirit dwells in her mantle of dust. But we are so faithless and material, that we lose half the education of this life, by not discerning God's teachings to us in the natural world, and the analogies there are between this nature, and His great master-work—the *soul*.

Look into thine own soul then. Here are mysteries more profound, more inexplicable, than in any chapter of nature's book. Here are the sacred wonders of scenery too! Except that in nature, there are no *discords;* all is harmony.

The soul has her darker side, her inconsistences, her incompletenesses—her *evil*. The soul, too, has her glacier wastes of spiritual decline and death, her flowerless deserts of unprofitable, unimproved opportunities. She has also her mountain scenery of aspiration, and her lone valleys of discontent, luxurious idleness, and unprofitable dreams. But the flowers typify the

Christian graces struggling on, trying to take firm root in the steril soil of unbelief, instability of purpose, weak resolve, and worldliness.

Hast thou then entered in vain into the "Treasures of the snow?"

Hast thou read in this Alpine scenery, the book of thine own soul?

Apply it then in all its wealth of imagery. So shall the mountains speak to thee of faith—the glacier-wastes, of spiritual death—the Alpine flower, of hope beyond the grave. Faith, Hope, and Love,—pointing to the Eternal Resurrection morn, this joyful Easter tide.

The Passing Bell.

"I am the resurrection and the life" saith the Lord, "he that believeth in me, though he were dead, yet shall he live: and whosoever liveth and believeth in me shall never die."—St. John xi. 25, 26.

"How shall I know thee in the sphere which keeps
The disembodied spirits of the dead;
When all of thee, that time could wither, sleeps,
And perishes among the dust we tread?

Will not thine own meek heart demand me there—
That heart whose fondest throbs to me were given;
My name on earth was ever in thy prayer,
And wilt thou never utter it in heaven?

In meadows, fanned by heaven's life-breathing wind,
In the resplendence of that glorious sphere,
And larger movements of the unfettered mind,
Wilt thou forget the love that joined us here?

The love that lived through all the stormy past,
And meekly with my harsher nature bore,
And deeper grew, and tenderer to the last;
Shall it expire with life, and be no more?

Shalt thou not teach me in that calmer home,
The wisdom that I learned so ill in this—
The wisdom which is love—till I become
Thy fit companion in that land of bliss?"

BRYANT.

The Passing Bell.

COLLECT FOR THE BURIAL SERVICE.

"O merciful God, the Father of our Lord Jesus Christ, who is the resurrection and the life; in whom whosoever believeth shall live, though he die; and whosoever liveth, and believeth in Him, shall not die eternally; who also hath taught us by His Holy Apostle Saint Paul, not to be sorry, as men without hope, for them that sleep in Him: We meekly beseech Thee, O Father, to raise us from the death of sin unto the life of righteousness; that, when we shall depart this life, we may rest in Him, as our hope is this our *brother* doth; and that, at the general Resurrection in the last day, we may be found acceptable in Thy sight; and receive that blessing, which Thy well-beloved Son shall then pronounce to all that love and fear Thee, saying, 'Come ye blessed children of my Father, receive the kingdom prepared for you from the beginning of the world :' Grant this we beseech Thee, O merciful Father, through Jesus Christ our Mediator and Redeemer. Amen."

TOLL on, in time with the raindrops that beat upon the window! The ivy too trembles under the impetuous fingering of the angry storm. It is the passing bell. Another soul has entered into rest, through the dream of the grave.

"The mourners go about the streets. The silver cord is loosed, the golden bowl is broken, the pitcher is broken at the fountain, the wheel broken at the cistern." The dust has returned to the earth as it was, and the spirit has returned to God who gave it.

How natural it is to cling to the cherished dust even after it is sculptured by death's cold remorseless fingers. Rather look up, and rejoice that the spirit has returned to God who gave it. Death had no power over that.

Shall we know each other after death? is the mourner's stifled utterance. If we walked less after the flesh, and more after the Spirit, we should scarcely *breathe* this question even mentally.

"The seed is not quickened except it die." To every seed its *own* body. Thus we are again figuratively taught the sublime doctrine of the resurrection.

Christ taught in symbols, and God has seen fit to shroud His glory and power in garments of metaphor, behind the hills of allegory.

And if we look into these symbols,

we shall perceive how lovely and convincing their teachings are.

The orientals still preserve this style of language to express their thoughts. King David tuned his harp to the same strain, and sang in figures, the Psalm of life:—"A span long," "a vain shadow," "the moth fretting the garment," "the grass that withereth," "the flower that fadeth."

So St. Paul employs the same style, pointing out the analogy between the celestial and terrestrial body, and the *identity* of each:—"As we have borne the image of the earthy, so shall we bear the image of the heavenly." "Behold, I shew you a mystery." It was as much a mystery to St. Paul, as it is to us, yet he believed and preached it.

But shall we know each other after death? Can we doubt this after the declaration that every seed will have its *own* body—its own identity perfectly recognisable? Yes—we shall know each other after death, more perfectly than we have ever known each other on earth, for then we shall no longer " see through a glass darkly, but face to face, then shall we know, even as we are known." Blessed thought, as we experience the utter instability of all we hold *here* only.

Strangers and Pilgrims we must confess ourselves to be, though there are many " caravanseras " on the way, where we meet, and hold sweet communion one with the other. Yet if we observe, we shall find sculptured over the porch of each of these "wayside Inns"—"*Vale.*"

But in the inner spiritual life there is an abiding joy and peace, though the heart's cry may be—" Shall we know each other after death?" Yes—if we have known each other here in the spirit.

St. Chrysostom says, "The axe is not laid to the leaves and branches, but to the root, not to the outward trimming of the tree of life, stripping it of its foliage, flowers and fruits; the root is cut, that which holds the soul to the earth from which it is so difficult to be weaned, even by sorrow."

Thus death—or what we call death—may strip us of the fruits, foliage, and flowers of what we love, but the root is only transplanted to the spiritual world.

There must be recognition after death, because of memory. Death is but "a change of raiment." There will be no difficulty in recognition, because of this change. "Christ is risen." Our eyes may be holden now, but "thanks be to God, which giveth us the victory through our Lord Jesus Christ."

> "Christ the Lord is risen to day,
> Sons of men and angels say;
> Raise your joys and triumphs high,—
> Sing ye heavens, and earth reply.
>
> Vain the stone, the watch, the seal,
> Christ has burst the gates of hell;
> Death in vain forbids him rise,
> Christ has opened paradise.
>
> Soar we now where Christ hath led,
> Following our exalted Head;
> Made like Him, like Him we rise;
> Ours the cross, the grave, the skies."

"If need be."

"There hath no temptation taken you, but such as is common to man: but God is faithful, who will not suffer you to be tempted above that ye are able; but will with the temptation also make a way to escape, that ye may be able to bear it."—1 Cor. x. 13.

"Alas! what hourly dangers rise,
What snares beset my way;
To Heaven, O let me lift mine eyes,
And hourly watch and pray.

Whene'er temptations fright my heart,
Or lure my feet aside;
My God, Thy powerful aid impart,
My Guardian and my Guide.

O keep me in Thy heavenly way,
And bid the tempter flee;
And let me never, never stray
From happiness and Thee."

"If need be."

"Wherein ye greatly rejoice, though now for a season, *if need be*, ye are in heaviness through manifold temptations: That the trial of your faith, being much more precious than of gold that perisheth, though it be tried with fire, might be found unto praise and honour and glory at the appearing of Jesus Christ."

1 Peter i. 6, 7.

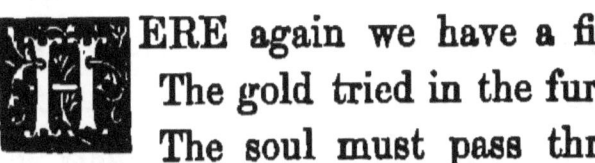ERE again we have a figure. The gold tried in the furnace. The soul must pass through her fiery ordeal to prove her faith, and her genuineness. It is her destiny sooner or later to be tried in the furnace of temptation—" Though now for

a season." She must then have her season of temptation.

Temptations are the test of the soul's allegiance to her God. Temptations must assail the citadel of the soul, notwithstanding that the banner of the Cross floats from her ramparts; notwithstanding that her sentinels are vigilant, and "watch unto prayer." Temptations will steal insidiously as scouts, and seek to undermine the foundation, though that foundation be built upon a rock. They will assume every guise to beguile and delude the most vigilant.

But let the citadel have one crevice large enough for a bird to enter, and she has lost her impregnability.

It is by keeping the moral and

spiritual edifice *complete*, that secures safety in defence.

Prayer should guard her entrance door. Occupation should build her workshop in the hall of entrance. Sloth, idleness, and selfishness, are the tools of evil spirits, which should be swept out like spiders and vermin from her threshold.

And yet, strive as we will, the silken snares of temptation are for ever entrapping us. Though gross forms of evil be repugnant to our taste and refinement, yet there are temptations that assume the garb of angels of light, to delude us in our spiritual walk—to seduce the soul from her allegiance to God.

The intellect is a world of temptation! How many great minds have, through intellect, been wrecked on the shoals of hopeless infidelity and death.

Genius carries an army of temptations in her regal train!

The heart often leads the soul away on the slippery pavement of temptation. Even religion may become a snare, if the faith is not "well grounded" and "established."

Temptation, as well as sorrow, brings the Christian often into heaviness.

It is a powerful instrument, though, in the chiselling of the moral edifice.

Who has not felt renewed in his strength, like an eagle, after having battled manfully with some wave of temptation; and instead of having been subdued, and drawn into a giddy whirlpool, has come out conqueror and more than conqueror, through Him that loved him?

Who has not in some period of his life, trembled on the brink of a precipice, perhaps dallied with the flowers that withered and died in his grasp, and was saved by the words of St. Paul whispering in his ear—"*If need be?*" And with his foot he has pushed off some great "rock of stumbling;" watched its increasing velocity and impetus, as it tore up the grass and flowers, till it spent its force in the valley mud below.

Yet this is a picture of many a soul, that has baffled the temptation that was sent but to try his faith.

It was the "need be." Christ's agony in the garden should weave its own mournful story in our hearts. He bore temptation, to shew us how to resist and grapple with it in every delusive form.

"Was any sorrow like unto my sorrow?" "I will make a way for thee to escape;" "Ye shall not be tempted above that ye are able," He whispers to us. Then let this Easter season—this Resurrection morn, which we celebrate, be indeed the spring-time of our faith.

Let the rose of Sharon, and the lily of the valleys be planted round the citadel of our hearts.

The rose to typify the splendour, the warmth, the love of Christ, our risen Lord.

The lily in her meek simplicity—the purity and sincerity of the Christian's life.

Do not drop this lily in the mud of earth, but twine it round the Easter rose.

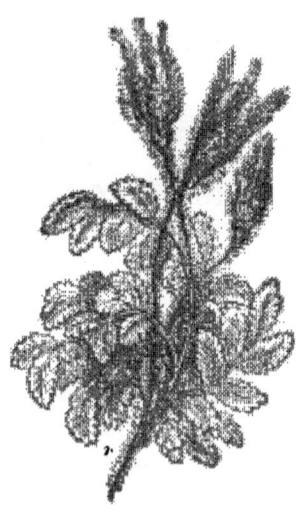

𝔄wake!

"Awake thou that sleepest, and arise from the dead, and Christ shall give thee light."—Eph. v. 14.

Awake! awake!—Why sleep the hours away?
Put on thy strength, and work while yet 'tis day,
That so as thou dost leave the charnel door,
Thy Christ on thee His glorious light may pour;
So thus armyed, leave all thy sins go by,
And rise with Him in endless unity.
Thou would'st not shame thy Master?—Then awake,
And Light's whole armour with thee faithful take;
Nor look behind on "earth's low tainted air,"—
Of sullen discontent—of pain—of care—
All sinks to nothing in that glorious Light,
That now would clothe thee in its garments white,
And shelter thee, till in the glowing skies,
Christ shall appear to greet thy longing eyes.

ALICE.

Awake!

"Awake, awake: Put on thy strength, O Zion; put on thy beautiful garments, O Jerusalem: shake thyself from the dust, and arise and sit down, O Jerusalem; loose thyself from the bands of thy neck, O captive daughter of Zion."

AWAKE, awake, dear friends, this Easter morn. Put on thy *beautiful garments*. The Lord is risen! Rise with Him. "Cast off the works of darkness, and put on the whole armour of light." As a bride cometh out from her chamber, so come

out from the past—its follies, mistakes, and graver sins; and bring with thee as offerings, this Easter morn, the roses of holier aspiration, purer thoughts, gentler affections, to deck the altar of our blessed faith.

Have we too, like Jerusalem, "been in the dust?" Then shake thy garments and arise. Have we been "chastened," "tried in the fire," and are we purified? Have we been running in the race set before us, and have we been the winners? Have we been purged with hyssop, and are we clean? Have we been washed, and are we whiter than the snow? Do "our garments smell of myrrh, aloes, and cassia;" and is our clothing of wrought gold?

Have we made the Lenten fast commemorative of our Lord's Passion and Cross? and have we also made it the funeral season of our sins? Are we awake with Christ, on this His resurrection morning? If so, we have already entered the ivory palace of our King.

Bring fresh roses, then, this Easter morning, wet with heavenly dew; bring the lily in her virgin purity, and lay them together at the foot of the Cross—meet emblems of our faith. "Shake thyself from the dust" of the past. Take off thy sackcloth, and "put on thy beautiful garments, O captive daughter of Zion;" for "instead of the thorn, shall come up the fir tree; and instead of the briar, shall come up the myrtle tree." "Thou art wearied in the greatness of thy way, yet saidst thou not,—*There is no hope.* Thou hast found the life of thine hand, therefore thou wast not grieved." "Enlarge then the place of thy tent, and let them stretch forth the curtains of thy habitations; spare not, lengthen thy cords, and strengthen thy stakes."

> "And nightly pitch thy moving tent,
> A day's march nearer home."

"I will make thy windows of agates, and thy gates of carbuncles, and all thy borders of pleasant stones." These are the promises that illuminate our Easter festival. These are the roses which we have gathered for you, fresh from the grave of our risen Lord.

They are fadeless and immortal, though they have blossomed from a Crown of Thorns, this Easter day.

Easter Day,
    March 27, 1864.

"He is not here, but is risen."
　　　　　　St. Luke xxiv. 6.

www.ingramcontent.com/pod-product-compliance
Lightning Source LLC
Chambersburg PA
CBHW022147160426
43197CB00009B/1470